Vocabulary

This book belongs to

....

Colour the star when you complete a page.
See how far you've come!

☆4 ☆5 ☆6 ☆7 ☆8 ☆9 ☆10 ☆11
☆12 ☆13 ☆14 ☆15 ☆16 ☆17 ☆18 ☆19
☆20 ☆21 ☆22 ☆23 ☆24 ☆25 ☆26 ☆27
☆28 ☆29 ☆30

Author: Shelley Welsh

How to use this book

- Your child will only need a writing pencil and some coloured crayons to be able to complete this book.
- Find a quiet, comfortable place to work, away from distractions.
- Help your child by reading the instructions and, where necessary, explain further what is needed to complete the task.
- Where there are topics, you will find a table with new vocabulary at the top of the page which links to the topic and/or experience. Encourage your child to read each word and check their understanding.
- Support your child to complete the task using the new vocabulary. This will reinforce their understanding.
- If an activity is too difficult for your child, move on to another page and return to it at a later stage. The activities should be challenging but also achievable. Children need to feel they are successful to be inspired to continue.
- Always end each activity on a positive note and before your child gets tired so they will be eager to return to the book next time. Learning should be fun and rewarding, not a chore.
- Help and encourage your child to check their own answers as they complete each activity.
- To embed the new vocabulary, encourage your child to use each word in a full sentence.
- An even better way to embed new vocabulary is to experience it in the wider world, for example, by travelling on the bus or train, visiting the hairdresser, going to the park or the beach. Have fun!
- Encourage your child to return to their favourite pages once they have been completed.
- Talk about the activities they enjoyed and what they have learnt.

Special features of this book

- **Progress chart:** when your child has completed a page, ask them to colour in the relevant star on the first page of the book. This will enable you to keep track of progress through the activities and help to motivate your child.
- **Familiar topics:** many topics should be relatable to things your child has seen or read about whilst possibly adding a few new words to extend their vocabulary.
- **Learning tips:** found throughout the book in a yellow box at the bottom of a page, these give you some suggested talking points based around the page topic. There is also an additional task should you wish to engage further with your child.

Published by Collins
An imprint of HarperCollins*Publishers* Ltd
The News Building
1 London Bridge Street
London
SE1 9GF

HarperCollins*Publishers*
Macken House, 39/40 Mayor Street Upper, Dublin 1
D01 C9W8, Ireland

Browse the complete Collins catalogue at
www.collins.co.uk

© HarperCollins*Publishers* Ltd 2023
First published 2023

10 9 8 7 6 5 4 3 2 1

ISBN 978-0-00-861789-9

The author asserts the moral right to be identified as the author of this work.

All rights reserved. No part of this publication may be reproduced, stored in a retrieval system, or transmitted, in any form or by any means, electronic, mechanical, photocopying, recording or otherwise, without the prior permission of Collins.

British Library Cataloguing in Publication Data

A Catalogue record for this publication is available from the British Library.

Author: Shelley Welsh
Publisher: Jennifer Hall
Project management and editorial: Chantal Addy
Design and layout: Sarah Duxbury and Contentra Technologies Ltd
All images: ©Shutterstock.com and ©HarperCollins*Publishers*
Cover design: Amparo Barrera and Sarah Duxbury
Production: Emma Wood
Printed in Great Britain by Martins the Printers

MIX
Paper | Supporting responsible forestry
FSC™ C007454

Contents

School is cool!	4
Food, glorious food!	6
Homophones	8
Near-homophones	10
Dictionary work	11
Planning a birthday party	12
Wild animals	14
Shape up!	16
Same or similar	18
Opposites attract	20
Word classes	22
General knowledge	23
Words of different origins	24
The Vikings	26
Definitions	28
Fun and games!	30
Answers	31

School is cool!

pencil	skirt	sharpener	library	equipment	laptop
uniform	homework diary	trousers	tie	mathematics	gym kit
geography	assembly	subjects	science	whiteboard	English
computer	history	tablet	trainers	exercise book	office

- Write the words of items from the grid above that you might **wear** in school.

    _____
    _____

- Write the words of things from the grid above that you might **use** in the classroom.

    _____
    _____
    _____
    _____

- Write the names of subjects from the grid above that you might **study** at school.

    _____
    _____

4

- Make up a timetable for a day at school.

Time	Lessons
	break time
	lunchtime
	home time

I can't wait until break!

I can't wait until lunchtime!

- What is your favourite lesson or activity at school, and why?

_____

_____

- What is your **least** favourite lesson or activity at school, and why?

_____

_____

Ask your child if they know why English is written with a capital E. Have a chat about other **proper nouns** – nouns that begin with a capital letter. Remind them that proper nouns include days of the week, months of the year, people's names, towns, countries and the names of places such as their school. Remind them that a capital letter is needed at the start of a sentence too.

Then ask them to independently write their name, their teacher's name and the name of their school.

5

Food, glorious food!

pasta	apples	soya milk	crisps	mangoes	beans
strawberries	vegetables	lentils	yoghurt	biscuits	chocolate
pineapples	cheese	potatoes	juice	cabbages	parsnips
onions	grapes	bread	fruit	peaches	cereal
fish	coconuts	bananas	carrots	fizzy drinks	pears

- Organise the items from the grid above that are **fruit** and **vegetables** into the correct columns below.

Fruit	Vegetables

Have a discussion with your child about healthy eating. Ask them which items in the vocabulary box would **not** form part of a healthy diet.

Can they tell you which items are dairy and which are carbohydrates?

- Answer the riddles. The answers can be found in the vocabulary box on page 6.

    I am a fruit that people like to crunch. _____

    You place something on me to make a sandwich. _____

    I am a vegetable that might make you cry! _____

    You might have me with milk for breakfast. _____

    Don't drink too much of me if you want healthy teeth. _____

    It's very hard to open me! _____

    Some people use me for a snowman's nose. _____

- Use the price tags on the food items to work out the answers to the following.

    | £1.50 per kg | £6.00 per kg | £2.50 per kg | £2.50 per 400g |

    Which item would cost you £3.00 for $\frac{1}{2}$ kg? _____

    Which item would cost you £3.00 for 2kg? _____

    Which item would cost you £5.00 for 800g? _____

    Which item would cost you £1.25 for $\frac{1}{2}$ kg? _____

    What is your total bill? _____

Homophones

main	mane	grate	great	here	hear
bear	bare	break	brake	fair	fare
berry	bury	peace	piece	knot	not
missed	mist	past	passed	groan	grown
to	two	too	rain	reign	rein

- Unscramble the letters to make a word, then next to it write the word that sounds the same but has a different spelling.

ogrnw

_____   _____

smdise

_____   _____

epice

_____   _____

yubr

_____   _____

8

- Complete the crossword using the clues below. Two are **not** in the vocabulary box on page 8.

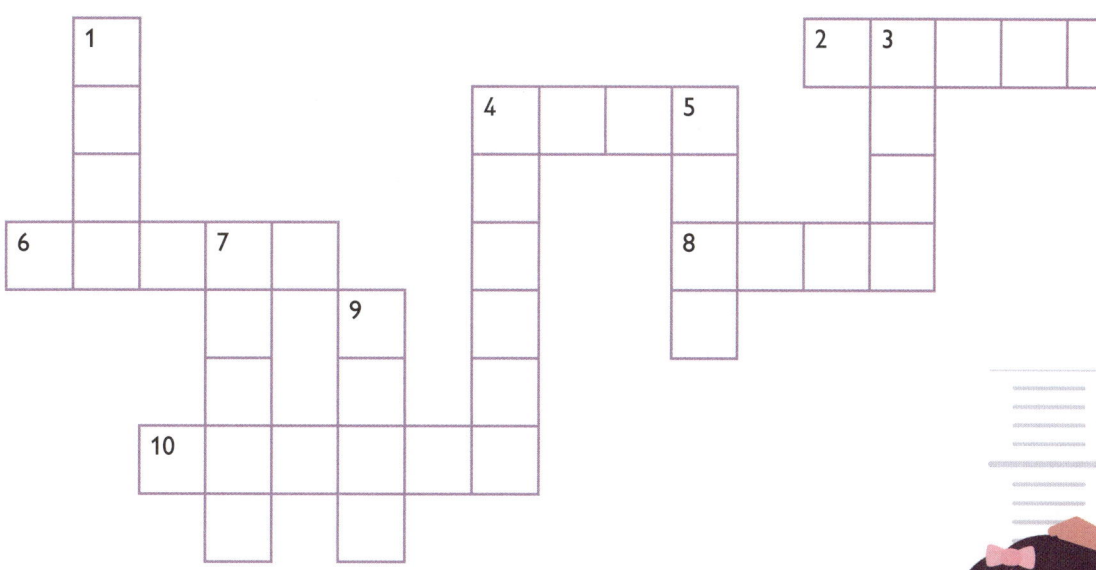

ACROSS

2. When you have become a bit taller

4. A light fog

6. To rule a country

8. Water from the sky

10. Past tense of pass

DOWN

1. Outer part of a bicycle wheel

3. A strap to guide a horse

4. Past tense of miss

5. When you start to lose energy

7. A noise you make when you have hurt yourself or are annoyed

9. A preposition

Remind your child that **homophones** are words that sound the same but have different spellings. Go over words such as **two**, **to** and **too** and **whose** and **who's**.

Can they make pairs of homophones with the following words?

meat → _____   not → _____   medal → _____   plain → _____

seen → _____   male → _____   fair → _____   weather → _____

Near-homophones

accept	except	affect	effect	quiet	quite
advice	advise	desert	dessert	won	one

- Choose the correct **near-homophone** from the vocabulary box to complete each sentence.

The home team _____ the match.

There is only _____ car left in the car park.

Matthew had to _____ that he was in the wrong.

Everyone had a partner _____ for Evie.

We were all _____ when the head teacher walked into the classroom.

Tarek's new computer was _____ expensive.

Pippa chose apple pie for _____.

Camels can be found in the _____.

Mr O'Rourke's new teaching method has had a positive _____ on us all.

Wilf tried not to let the teasing _____ him.

I asked Mum for some _____ about my homework.

Mal asked his coach to _____ him about his exercise regime.

Remind your child that **near-homophones** are words that sound *almost* the same but have different spellings, and are therefore easily confused.

Can they create sentences of their own using the near-homophones in the vocabulary box above?

Dictionary work

- Use the alphabet to help you place the words in each row in alphabetical order and then check using a dictionary.

A B C D E F G H I J K L M N O P Q R S T U V W X Y Z

| potato | position | pressure | particular | perhaps |

| surprise | special | separate | sentence | strange |

| extreme | enough | exercise | early | eight |

| appear | arrive | address | accident | apple |

- Use your dictionary to find a word that comes **between** each of the following words. Write the definition of the word you choose.

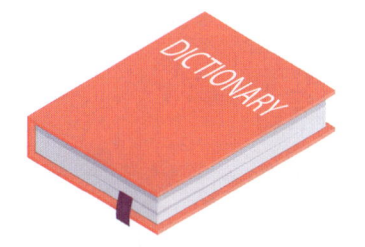

	Word	Definition
spoil sport		
calm clap		
temple tender		
zero zoom		
graffiti graph		

11

Planning a birthday party

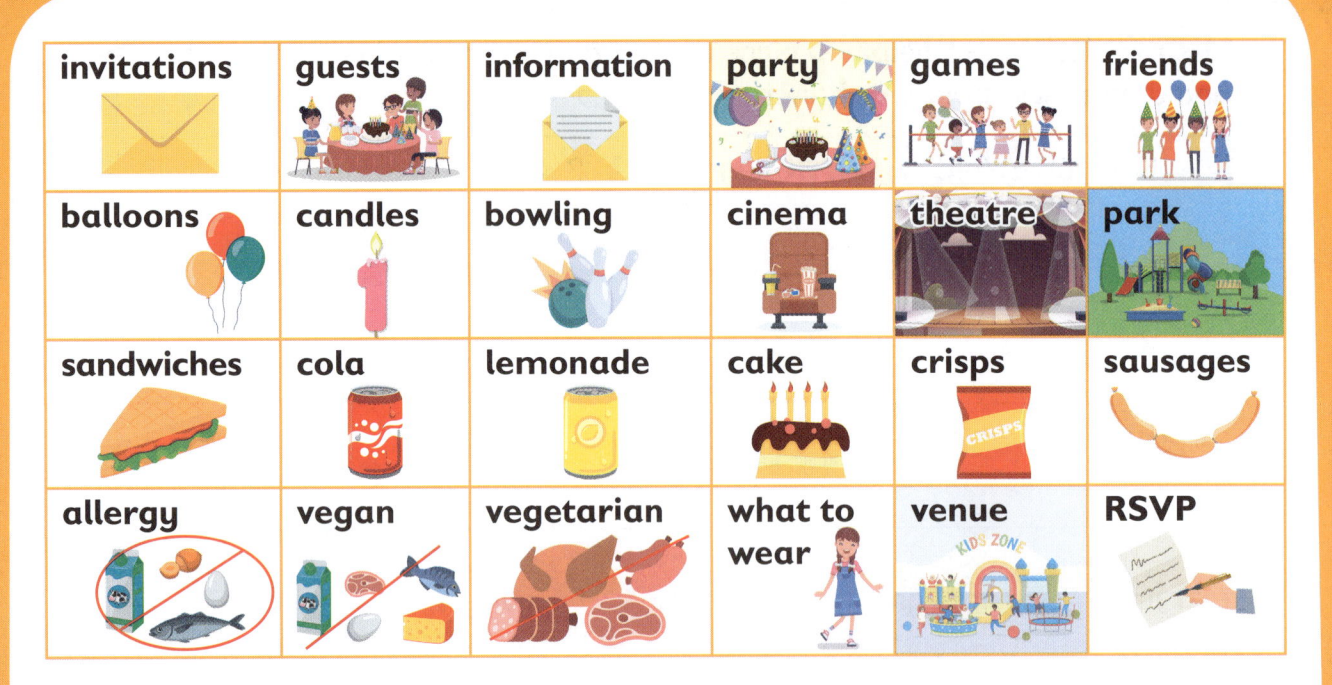

invitations	guests	information	party	games	friends
balloons	candles	bowling	cinema	theatre	park
sandwiches	cola	lemonade	cake	crisps	sausages
allergy	vegan	vegetarian	what to wear	venue	RSVP

- Complete the party invitation below. Use the checklist to help you. Draw some artwork on your invitation.
    - o Your name
    - o Your guest's name
    - o Venue information
    - o What to wear
    - o Start time
    - o Finish time
    - o Include a phone number to reply to

_____

would like to invite

_____

to a party!

_____
_____
_____

Explain to your child that **RSVP** often appears on an invitation and that it means 'please reply' (from the French *Répondez s'il vous plaît*) and that a **venue** is a place where something happens.

Ask them why it is important to receive a reply from everyone who is given an invitation. Why might their guests want to know the **dress code** and why might they need to let you know about a food **allergy** or whether they are **vegan** or **vegetarian**?

- Find the seven food and drink words that you might have at a party in the wordsearch below. Two are **not** in the vocabulary box on page 12. Write the words on the lines below.

s	s	a	n	d	w	i	c	h	e	s
y	v	x	c	o	l	a	g	t	h	j
i	c	e	c	r	e	a	m	r	a	e
j	g	a	p	p	i	v	m	i	n	l
t	j	c	a	k	e	s	z	s	m	l
w	w	c	b	o	p	f	p	p	z	y
c	s	a	u	s	a	g	e	s	c	x

_____   _____

_____   _____

_____   _____

_____

- Unscramble the jumbled letters in bold and write the correct word on the line next to each.

Keira has sent ten **taitnviiosn** _____ to her friends, inviting them

to her **arypt** _____. The **evune** _____ is the **rpka** _____ where they

will have a **cpnici** _____. There will be **asnhidswce** _____,

loedemna _____, **asageus** _____ rolls and

a **ekac** _____. The **sders cdeo** _____

_____ is jeans and waterproof coats, just in case it rains.

Two of Keira's friends have a nut **gyaller** _____

and one is a **angetveari** _____.

13

Wild animals

elephant	robin	tiger	lion	zebra	shark
owl	eagle	goose	fox	orangutan	badger
penguin	panda	kangaroo	lizard	snake	whale
dolphin	giraffe	duck	monkey	cheetah	hawk

- Fill in the missing letters to make the names of wild animals.

• Complete the sentences using the pictures to help you.

I live in Asia and have big _____.

I am an _____.

I carry my _____ in my pouch.

I am a _____.

I have a long _____ and I am tall.

I am a _____.

My colours are _____ and _____ and I live in the Antarctic.

I am a _____.

I am the fastest land animal in the _____.

I am a _____.

I am a mammal who lives in the _____.

I am a _____.

Chat with your child about their favourite animals. Ask them about the different features of mammals and reptiles and discuss their habitats. Support them to use the internet to research.

Ask your child to classify the animals listed below according to whether they are vertebrates (have a backbone) or invertebrates (no backbone): butterflies, blackbirds, spiders, crocodiles, worms, buffalo

15

Shape up!

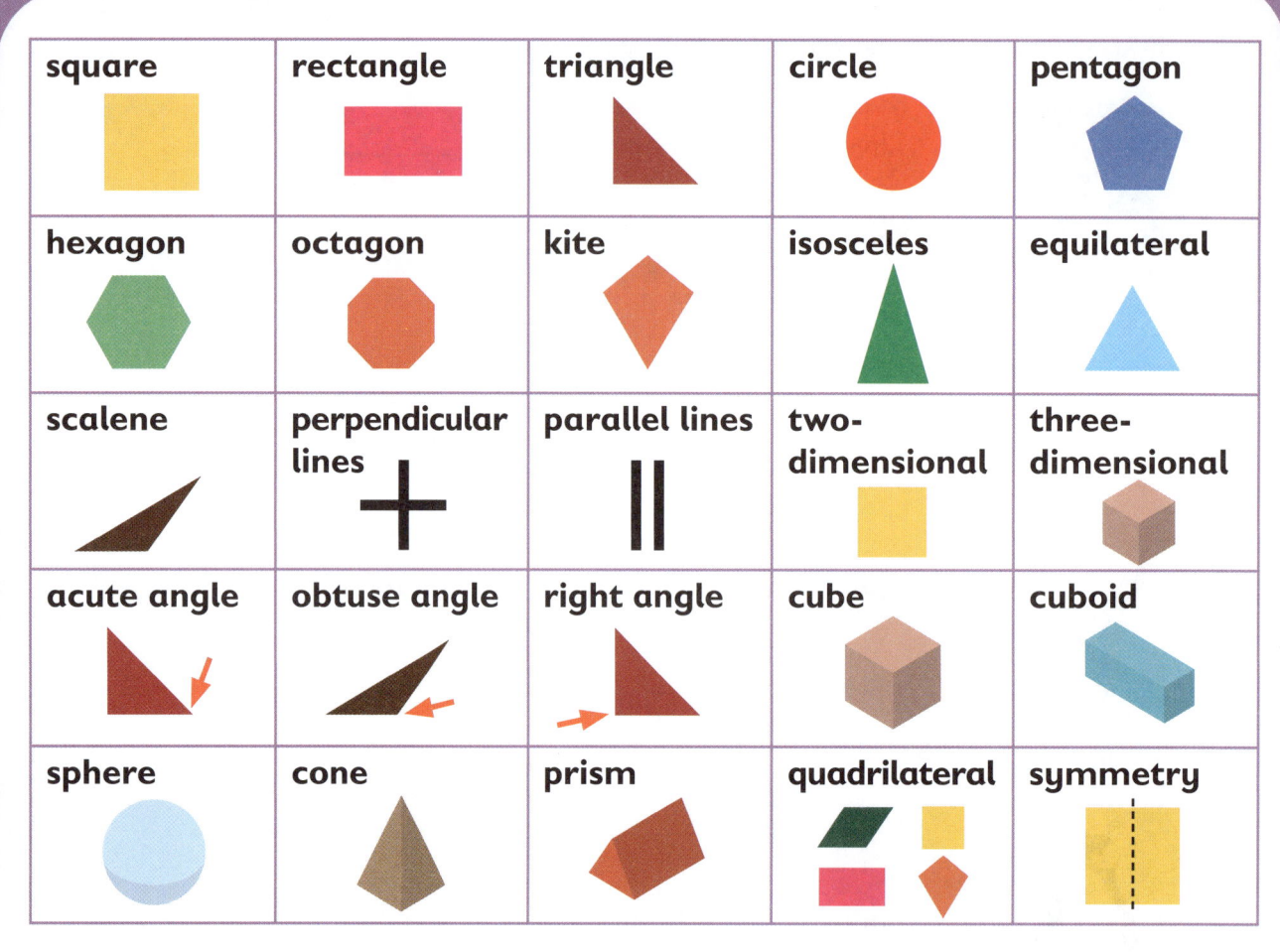

square	rectangle	triangle	circle	pentagon
hexagon	octagon	kite	isosceles	equilateral
scalene	perpendicular lines	parallel lines	two-dimensional	three-dimensional
acute angle	obtuse angle	right angle	cube	cuboid
sphere	cone	prism	quadrilateral	symmetry

- Label each two-dimensional (2-D) shape.

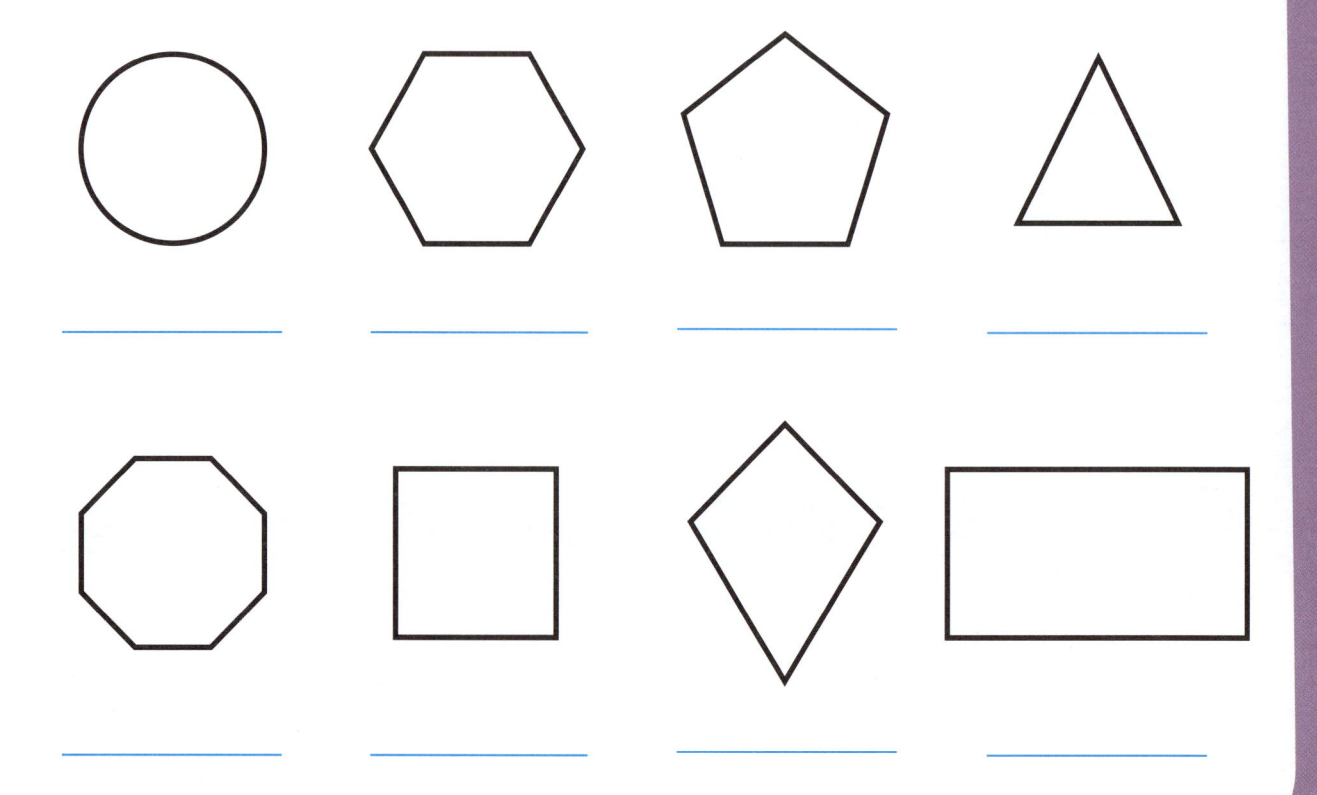

- Find a word (or words) hidden inside each of these words. One has been done for you.

symmetry	met try	sphere	_____
prism	_____	cone	_____
quadrilateral	_____	obtuse	_____
rectangle	_____	acute	_____
perpendicular	_____	cube	_____
pentagon	_____		

- Solve these shape riddles.

I have 1 curved edge. _____

There are 2 of me and we never meet. _____

I have 3 sides the same length. _____

I have 6 faces, 12 edges and 8 vertices. _____

I am less than 90°. _____

I have 6 sides. _____

Help your child remember shape facts: A **tri**cycle has 3 wheels; a **tri**angle has 3 sides. A **quad** bike has 4 wheels; a **quad**rilateral is a 4-sided shape. An **oct**opus has 8 legs; an **oct**agon has 8 sides.

Challenge your child to draw and label an **equilateral triangle** (all sides the same length), an **isosceles triangle** (two sides the same length), a **scalene triangle** (no equal sides), and a **right-angled triangle**.

17

Same or similar

- Draw a line to match each word to one that has the same or a similar meaning.

probably	tiny
separate	protect
reign	escort
minute	unconnected
increase	finish
complete	raise
answer	likely
naughty	odd
peculiar	significant
purpose	well-liked
guard	reply
guide	rule
popular	goal
important	disobedient

- Replace the words in bold with a suitable alternative. Use a thesaurus to help you.

"You're very late," **moaned** _____ Mia's football coach. "I'm a bit **cross** _____ with you because it keeps happening."

"I'm **really tired** _____," **replied** _____ Mia. "So, I slept through my alarm. **Sadly**, _____, I missed the bus and had to walk."

"OK. Join the others as **fast** _____ as you can. This is a really **important** _____ game!"

Without **delay**, _____, Mia **ran** _____ towards the pitch.

She had **thought** _____ she would be sitting on the bench for the first half!

Help your child understand how using **synonyms** – words that have the same or similar meaning – can make their writing more interesting. Rather than repeating a word, they could use a thesaurus to find an alternative. However, help them to see that not all words offered in a thesaurus will work in the same context!

Ask your child to use a thesaurus to find synonyms for the following words:

possibly   disappear
remember   occasionally

Opposites attract

- Replace the words in bold with their opposite meaning. Use a thesaurus to help you.

    Xavier has **started** _____ his homework.

    The climbers **failed** _____ in their mission to reach the top.

    The maths test turned out to be very **easy** _____.

    Yolande's new dog is very **well-behaved** _____.

    The ceremony was a very **public** _____ affair.

    Finn gave a **factual** _____ recount of events.

- Find the words in the wordsearch that have the opposite meaning to the highlighted words. Write each pair of words on the lines next to the wordsearch.

s	m	o	l	d	i	c	h	e	a
n	e	w	b	l	a	g	o	f	f
c	l	c	e	e	a	h	r	r	t
c	t	p	f	s	t	a	l	e	e
o	c	s	o	f	t	e	s	s	r
m	c	f	r	e	e	z	e	h	y
e	a	u	e	a	h	a	r	d	x

_____ _____

_____ _____

_____ _____

_____ _____

_____ _____

Play a game with your child where you say a word and they give you its opposite meaning. Make sure the word class is the same – if your word is an adjective, their word needs to be an adjective; if your word is a verb, their word needs to be a verb, etc. You can find the opposite meaning of a word in a thesaurus.

Here are some words you might use:
slow   early   hide   rough
luckily   accept   full

20

- Draw a line to match each **prefix** to a word on the right to make its opposite meaning.

un	behave
mis	active
in	septic
ir	possible
il	happy
im	responsible
anti	legal

- Solve the clues by adding a **prefix** with a negative or opposite meaning to each of the following words.

mature	responsible	agree
literate	social	obedient

Not very sociable _____

Unable to read or write _____

Behaving childishly _____

When you don't follow the rules _____

Careless or thoughtless _____

Differ in opinion _____

Word classes

> A dictionary tells you the class of each word. For example, whether it is a noun, adjective, adverb, verb, preposition or conjunction.

- Use your dictionary to help you find the word class of each of the following.

Word	Word class
pest	
slippery	
hibernate	
describe	
although	
culture	
at	
finally	

- Some words have more than one word class.

Word	Word class 1	Word class 2
coat		
brake		
envy		
before		
group		

- Write how many different word classes you can find for the word **fine**.

_____

_____

General knowledge

- Complete the words using the clues.

  Enormous, pointed structures built in Egypt. p _ _ _ _ _ s

  Humans, animals and plants cannot live without this. _ o _ _ _ _

  Percussion instruments that you bang together. c _ _ _ _ s

  This month has 29 days in a leap year. F _ _ _ _ _ _ _

- Draw a line to link the **collective noun** on the left with its correct pair on the right.

a swarm of	ants
a flock of	flowers
a bunch of	bees
a bouquet of	birds
an army of	grapes

- Answer these quick quiz questions.

  What kind of food is spaghetti? _____

  In which country might you find a platypus and a wombat? _____

  Write the months of the year that have 30 days.

  _____

  _____

23

Words of different origins

The word endings **gue** and **que** are French in origin. The **ue** is not pronounced.

- Solve the clues to complete the words.

A widespread disease in Tudor times.   p _ _ _ _ _

Only one or very special.   u _ _ _ _ _

A body part you taste with.   t _ _ _ _ _

A place of prayer for Muslims.   m _ _ _ _ _

A conversation between two people.   d _ _ _ _ _ _ _

Chat with your child about other words we use that have a foreign origin, for example champagne and patio.

Work with them to find the country of origin of each of the following words:

caravan   karaoke   technique   moustache

24

- Draw a line to match each word of foreign origin with its meaning.

silhouette	a shop where medicines are sold
graffiti	a small wooden house
paparazzi	someone who cooks in a restaurant
chef	the outline of a dark shape seen against a light background
chalet	independent photographers who take pictures of celebrities
chemist	artwork written, painted or drawn on a wall

- Use your dictionary or the internet to find the origins and definitions of these words that we use in English.

ballet _____

tsunami _____

safari _____

catalogue _____

genre _____

- Write a sentence containing the word **catalogue** to show you understand its meaning.

_____

_____

The Vikings

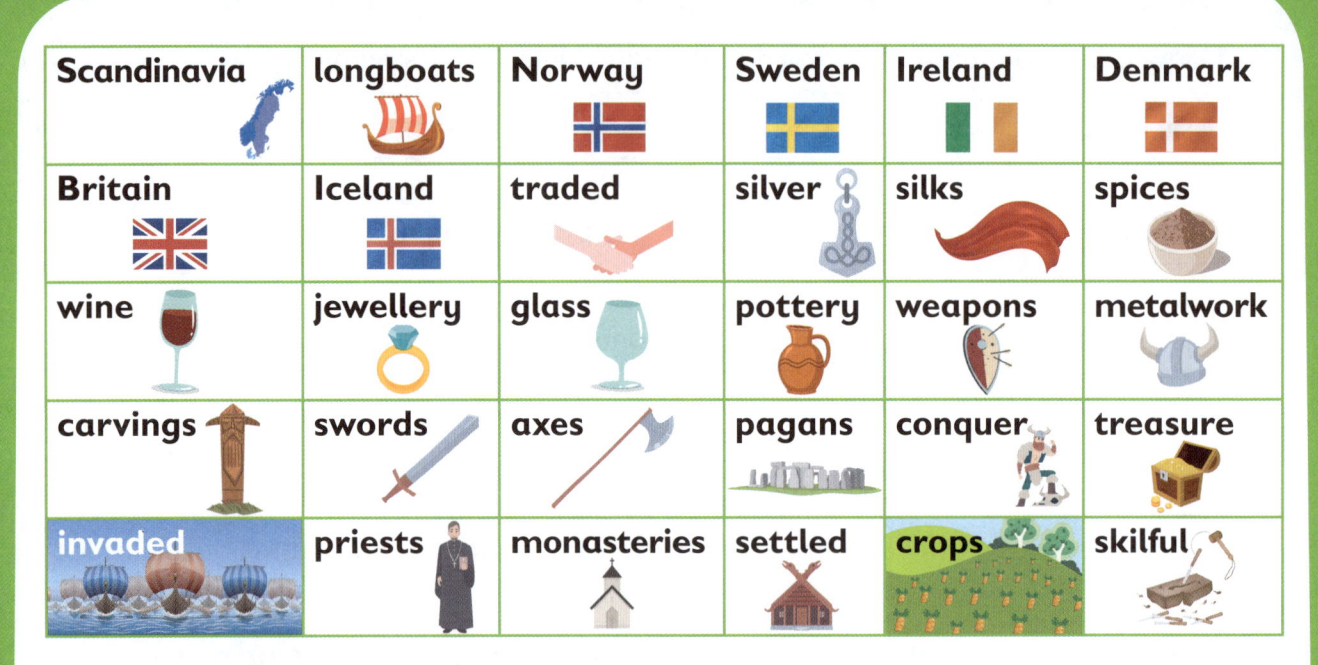

Scandinavia	longboats	Norway	Sweden	Ireland	Denmark
Britain	Iceland	traded	silver	silks	spices
wine	jewellery	glass	pottery	weapons	metalwork
carvings	swords	axes	pagans	conquer	treasure
invaded	priests	monasteries	settled	crops	skilful

- Complete the passage using the words in the vocabulary box.

The Viking age was from about 700 to 1100 CE. Vikings came to B_____ and I_____, travelling by l_____, from their homes in N_____, S_____ and D_____ in S_____.

Vikings t_____ in goods such as s_____, s_____, s_____, w_____, j_____, g_____ and p_____.

In around 787 CE, the Vikings i_____ Britain, using w_____ such as a_____ and long s_____.

The Vikings were pagans, meaning they were not Christians like most people in Britain at the time. They stole t_____ owned by the p_____ who lived in m_____.

Some Vikings came to Britain to settle peacefully. They grew c_____ and were s_____ at crafting beautiful m_____ and wooden c_____.

- Underline the words in the text below that should have been written with a capital letter. Remember: you need a capital letter at the start of a sentence and for proper nouns.

> in 865 CE, an army of vikings sailed across the north sea to britain where they intended to conquer the land rather than raid it.
>
> over several years, the viking army waged battles throughout northern england and took control of the anglo-saxon kingdoms of northumbria, east anglia and most of mercia.
>
> by 878 CE, almost all the kingdoms had fallen to the vikings. all apart from wessex, which was ruled by king alfred the great. king alfred beat the vikings in battle but was unable to drive them out of britain.

- Answer these questions about the passage above. Write your answers in full sentences.

Where did the Vikings sail in 865 CE?

_____

Which kingdoms did the Vikings take over?

_____

Who beat the Vikings in battle?

_____

A proper noun is a specific name for a particular person, place or thing. Other proper nouns include days of the week, months of the year, and book and film titles. Ask your child to find the proper nouns in the words listed below:

thursday   garden   mrs morris
   king charles iii   saturn
london   park lane primary school
      summer   annie

Remind your child that an initial capital letter is not joined to the next letter.

Ask your child to write their full name and address, ensuring they have used capital letters appropriately.

27

Definitions

- Use your dictionary or the internet to find a definition for each of the following words. Remember: some words can have more than one definition!

    natural   _____

    increase   _____

    pressure   _____

    extreme   _____

    reign   _____

    sombre   _____

    devour   _____

- Write a sentence containing one of the words above.

    _____

    _____

A **glossary** can usually be found at the back of an information book. It gives definitions of words (sometimes written in bold or underlined) found in the information text.

Read an information text with your child. As you come across each word in bold (or underlined) that features in the glossary, discuss with your child what it might mean before referring to the glossary.

- Use an information book or the internet to help you complete this glossary that you might find in a book about volcanoes.

Glossary

magma _____

lava _____

mantle _____

extinct _____

dormant _____

tectonic plates _____

- Using the glossary words above and either an information book or the internet, write a short paragraph about volcanoes.

_____

Fun and games!

- Find the four-letter word hidden at the end of one word and the beginning of the next. Write the word. One has been done for you.

    I like to be out in the fresh air.   hair

    Mum adores trekking in the hills.   _____

    A stitch in time saves nine.   _____

    The clouds on the horizon eclipsed our view. _____

- Underline one word in the first set of words and another in the second set that are linked to each other.

    (peaches   farmer   sheep)   (town   smell   fruit)

    (lungs   heart   unwell)   (breathe   sleep   pillow)

    (hexagon   pentagon   triangle)   (four   seven   five)

- Write the word (or words) you can find in each of the following words. For example: breathe **at, eat, the, breath**

    consider _____   fright _____   attract _____

    bleary _____   increase _____   splurge _____

    feather _____   stable _____   sailor _____

- How many words can you make from the following letters?

    E   F   D   I   H   I   S   N

    _____

    _____

    _____

30

Answers

Page 4
- skirt, uniform, trousers, tie, gym kit, trainers
- pencil, sharpener, library, equipment, laptop, homework diary, whiteboard, computer, tablet, exercise book
- mathematics, geography, science, English, history

Page 5
- Timetables will vary. Example:

Time	Lessons
09:00	maths
10:00	English
11:00	break time
11:15	art
12:30	science
1:15	lunchtime
2:15	geography
3:15	home time

- A sentence saying favourite lesson or activity and why.
- A sentence saying least favourite lesson or activity and why.

Page 6

Fruit	Vegetables
apples	beans
mangoes	potatoes
strawberries	cabbage
pineapples	parsnips
grapes	onions
peaches	carrots
coconut	
bananas	
pears	

Page 7
- apple, bread, onion, cereal, juice/fizzy drinks, coconut, carrot
- strawberries, onions, cheese, potatoes; total bill = £12.25

Page 8
- grown, groan; missed, mist; piece, peace; bury, berry

Page 9
- Crossword: TYRE; GROWN; MISS; REIGN; RAIN; PINE; ROAD; PASSED
- meat → meet; not → knot; medal → meddle; plain → plane; seen → scene; male → mail; fair → fare; weather → whether

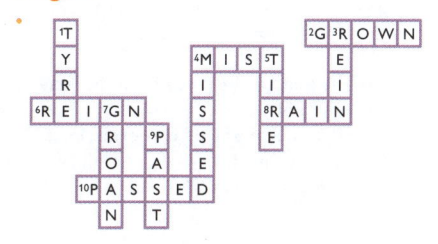

Page 10
- won; one; accept; except; quiet; quite; dessert; desert; effect; affect; advice; advise

Page 11
- Alphabetical order:
  particular perhaps position potato pressure sentence separate special strange surprise early eight enough exercise extreme accident address appear apple arrive
- Child to write words and their definitions.

Page 12
- Invitations will vary. Example:

  Keira would like to invite Mohammed to a party!
  Venue: The Bowling Alley, Patterton
  Start time: 2:00pm
  Finish time: 5:00pm
  What to wear: Fancy dress!
  RSVP: Keira's mum 01234 567891

Page 13
- sandwiches, cola, ice cream, cakes, sausages, jelly, crisps
- invitations; party; venue; park; picnic; sandwiches; lemonade; sausage; cake; dress code; allergy; vegetarian

Page 14
- Crossword with: giraffe, panda, goose, elephant, penguin, eagle, hawk, badger, zebra, snake, tiger, robin

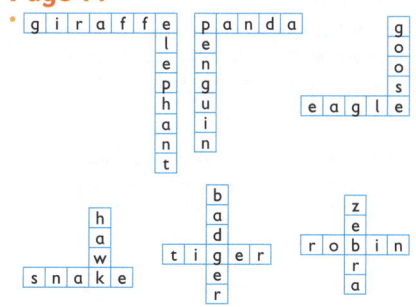

Page 15
- I live in Asia and have big **ears**. I am an **elephant**.
  I carry my **baby** in my pouch. I am a **kangaroo**.
  I have a long **neck** and I am tall. I am a **giraffe**.
  My colours are **black** and **white** and I live in the Antarctic. I am a **penguin**.
  I am a mammal who lives in the **sea**. I am a **dolphin**.
  I am the fastest land animal in the **world**. I am a **cheetah**.

Page 16
- Each shape correctly labelled: circle, hexagon, pentagon, triangle, octagon, square, kite, rectangle

Page 17
- **sphere:** her/here/he; **prism:** is; **cone:** on/one/con; **quadrilateral:** late/ate/later/era/quad; **obtuse:** use/us; **rectangle:** an/tan/angle/tangle; **acute:** cut/cute; **perpendicular:** pen/pend/end; **cube:** cub/be; **pentagon:** pen/tag/on/ago
- circle; parallel lines; equilateral triangle; cube/cuboid; acute angle; hexagon

Page 18
- probably — likely
- separate — unconnected
- reign — rule
- minute — tiny
- increase — raise
- complete — finish
- answer — reply
- naughty — disobedient
- peculiar — odd
- purpose — goal
- guard — protect
- guide — escort
- popular — well-liked
- important — significant

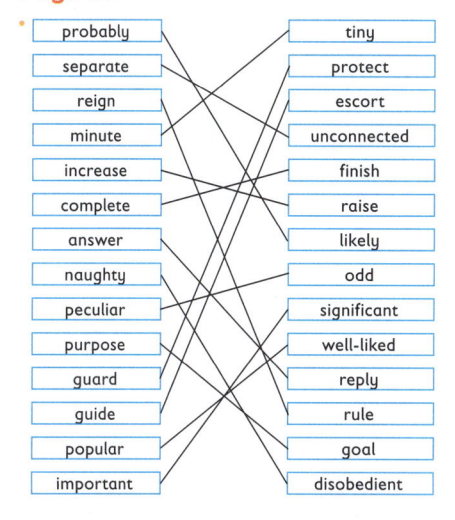

Page 19
- Answers will vary.
  grumbled; annoyed; exhausted; responded; Unfortunately; quickly; crucial; hesitation; rushed; imagined

Page 20
- finished; succeeded; difficult; naughty; private; fictitious
- Wordsearch containing: old, new, soft, freeze, hard
- melt — freeze
- new — old
- after — before
- stale — fresh
- hard — soft
- go — come

Page 21

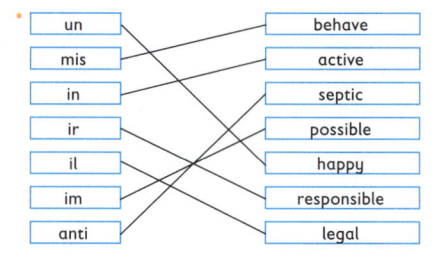

un	—	behave
mis	—	active
in	—	septic
ir	—	possible
il	—	happy
im	—	responsible
anti	—	legal

- antisocial/anti-social; illiterate; immature; disobedient; irresponsible; disagree

Page 22

- Answers will vary according to the dictionary used.

Word	Word class
pest	noun
slippery	adjective
hibernate	verb
describe	verb
although	conjunction
culture	noun (abstract)/verb
at	preposition
finally	adverb

Word	Word class 1	Word class 2
coat	noun	verb
brake	noun	verb
envy	noun	verb
before*	adverb	conjunction
group	noun	verb

*before can also be a preposition
- fine: verb, noun, adjective

Page 23

- pyramids; oxygen; cymbals; February

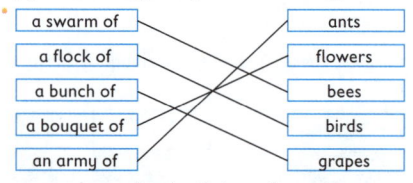

a swarm of	—	ants
a flock of	—	flowers
a bunch of	—	bees
a bouquet of	—	birds
an army of	—	grapes

- pasta; Australia; April, June, September, November

Page 24

- plague; unique; tongue; mosque; dialogue

Page 25

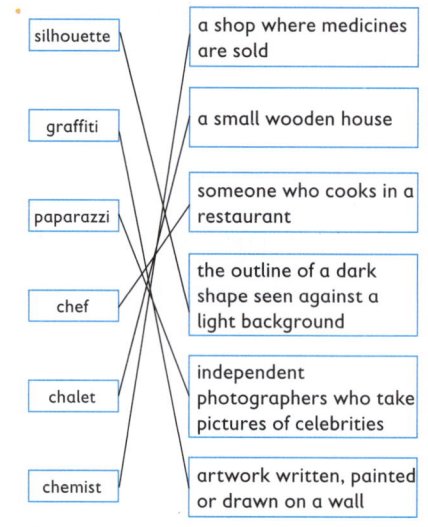

silhouette	—	a shop where medicines are sold
graffiti	—	a small wooden house
paparazzi	—	someone who cooks in a restaurant
chef	—	the outline of a dark shape seen against a light background
chalet	—	independent photographers who take pictures of celebrities
chemist	—	artwork written, painted or drawn on a wall

- Answers will vary depending on dictionary or internet site used. Examples:
ballet – skilled dancing with carefully planned movements
tsunami – a very large wave, often caused by an earthquake, that flows onto the land and destroys things
safari – a trip to observe wild animals
catalogue – as a verb, to list a series of similar events or qualities; as a noun, a list of things such as the goods you can buy from a company
genre – a particular type of literature, painting, music, film, or other art form

- Accept a suitable sentence which shows understanding of the meaning of the word **catalogue** as either a verb or a noun.

Page 26

- Britain; Ireland; longboats; Norway; Sweden; Denmark; Scandinavia; traded; silver; silks; spices; wine; jewellery; glass; pottery; invaded; weapons; axes; swords; treasure; priests; monasteries; crops; skilful; metalwork; carvings

Page 27

- The words in bold should have been written with an initial capital letter as they are either the first word in a sentence or a proper noun:

  in 865 CE, an army of **vikings** sailed across the **north sea** to **britain** where they intended to conquer the land rather than raid it.

  over several years, the **viking** army waged battles throughout northern **england** and took control of the **anglo-saxon** kingdoms of **northumbria**, **east anglia** and most of **mercia**.

  by 878 CE, almost all the kingdoms had fallen to the **vikings**. **all** apart from **wessex**, which was ruled by **king alfred the great**. **king alfred** beat the **vikings** in battle but was unable to drive them out of **britain**.

- Answers to questions about the passage may vary. Ensure proper nouns in answers start with a capital letter.

  The Vikings sailed to Britain in 865 CE.
  The Vikings took over the kingdoms of Northumbria, East Anglia and most of Mercia.
  King Alfred the Great beat the Vikings.

Page 28

- Definitions will vary depending on the dictionary used.
- Sentences will vary depending on the word chosen.

Page 29

- magma – molten rock that is formed in very hot conditions inside the Earth
lava – the very hot liquid rock that comes out of a volcano
mantle – the part of the Earth between the crust and the core
extinct – describes a volcano that no longer erupts or is not expected to erupt again
dormant – describes a volcano that has not erupted in a long time but is expected to erupt again in the future
tectonic plates – gigantic pieces of the Earth's crust and uppermost mantle

- Answer will vary. Check for accurate use of vocabulary.

Page 30

- Mum ado**res t**rekking in the hills. (rest)
A sti**tch in** time saves nine. (chin)
The clouds on the hori**zon e**clipsed our view. (zone)

- The underlined words are associated with each other.
(<u>peaches</u>   farmer   sheep)
(town   smell   <u>fruit</u>)
(<u>lungs</u>   heart   unwell)
(<u>breathe</u>   sleep   pillow)
(hexagon   <u>pentagon</u>   triangle)
(four   seven   <u>five</u>)

- consider → side, con
fright → right, rig
attract → at, act, tract
bleary → ear
increase → ease, in, crease
splurge → urge
feather → eat, at, feat, the, her
stable → able, tab, table
sailor → ail, sail

- 24 words that can be made from the letters E F D I H I S N:
finished, finish, fin, shed, he, she, his, in, din, dish, sin, shin, fine, find, dine, hind, shine, fish, fed, hid, end, send, die, den